W9-DDJ-287

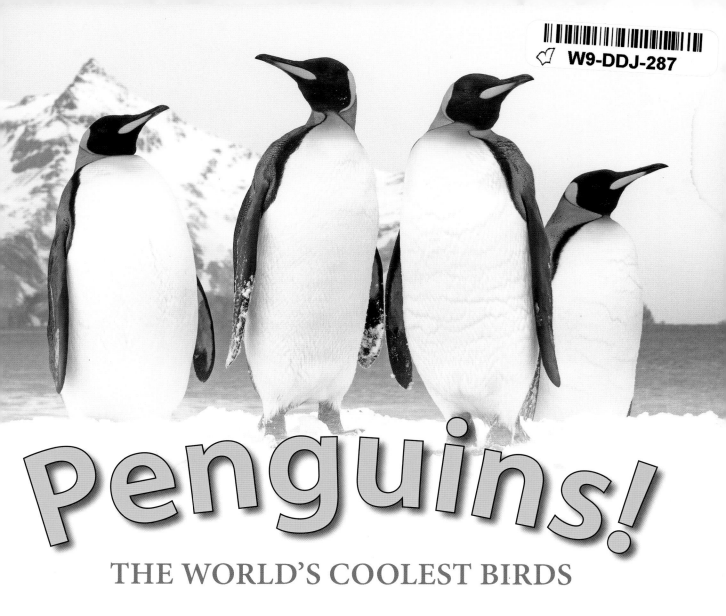

Penguins!

THE WORLD'S COOLEST BIRDS

Text and Photography
WAYNE LYNCH

FIREFLY BOOKS

A FIREFLY BOOK

Published by Firefly Books Ltd. 2016

Copyright © 2016 Firefly Books Ltd.
Text copyright © 2016 Wayne Lynch
Photographs copyright © 2016 Wayne Lynch except the following: African –
Frank Todd (p.73), Northern Rockhopper (penguin #1) – Rinie Van Meurs,
Fiordland (penguin #4) and African (penguin #12) – Frank Todd (p.77)

All rights reserved. No part of this publication may be reproduced, stored in
a retrieval system, or transmitted in any form or by any means, electronic,
mechanical, photocopying, recording or otherwise, without the prior written
permission of the Publisher.

First printing

Publisher Cataloging-in-Publication Data (U.S.)
A CIP record for this title is available from the Library of Congress

Library and Archives Canada Cataloguing in Publication
A CIP record for this title is available from Library and Archives Canada

Published in the United States by
Firefly Books (U.S.) Inc.
P.O. Box 1338, Ellicott Station
Buffalo, New York 14205

Published in Canada by
Firefly Books Ltd.
50 Staples Avenue, Unit 1
Richmond Hill, Ontario L4B 0A7

Cover and interior design: Kimberley Young

Printed in China

The publisher gratefully acknowledges the financial support for our publishing
program by the Government of Canada through the Canada Book Fund as
administered by the Department of Canadian Heritage.

Acknowledgments

Field biologists often work under difficult conditions, driven by their quest to understand the natural world and the fascinating wild creatures that live in it. In my research on penguins, I spent hundreds of wonderful hours reading the scholarly words of field biologists. These dedicated men and women helped me to understand the world of penguins, and I am indebted to them all.

This is my seventh book with the friendly, capable folks at Firefly Books. As before, working with them has been an easy and pleasurable task. I owe special thanks to publisher Lionel Koffler, editor Michael Mouland, copy editor Beverley Sotolov and designer Kimberley Young.

Finally, this is my 58th book all told, and for the 58th time, I would like to dedicate it to the most deserving person in my life — my wife of 41 years, Aubrey Lang. At the risk of repeating myself, she is the most interesting, stimulating, loving, compassionate, unselfish person I know. I love her dearly.

A chinstrap may stretch and yawn after a preening session.

For Aubrey, as always

3

Adélie penguins
(*Pygoscelis adeliae*),
Orne Islands,
Antarctic Peninsula

Contents

What Is a Penguin? 8

What's on the Menu? 30

Penguin Killers 56

Problems in Penguinland 72

Penguins in Motion 22

The Mating Game 40

Parting Penguins 66

Introduction

To cool off, an Adélie raises its flippers to expose the lightly feathered undersides.

I've traveled to the sparkling ice and snow of Antarctica a dozen times. On one of my earliest trips I went ashore at a huge Adélie penguin colony, where 125,000 pairs of black-and-whites nested from the shoreline to the tops of every ridge. I wandered around the colony for nearly 12 hours; it was one of the most enjoyable penguin-watching days I have ever had.

No matter where I looked in the colony, penguins were on the move: tobogganing over the glistening snow on their bulging bellies, porpoising through the silver water like star-studded dolphins and waddling up slopes of rock with their flippers bouncing. There were penguins screaming and fighting with their neighbors, while others offered gifts of precious pebbles to their mates. Still others warmed and fed their wobbly-necked young. I laughed again and again when the nesting birds carelessly blasted each other with sloppy, pink guano.

My best experience, however, came at the end of the day. I sat on a shelf of ice along the shoreline and watched gangs of penguins leap out of the water like rockets — who says penguins can't fly. One soaring bird miscalculated its approach and landed squarely in my lap. With an indignant squawk, the startled penguin tumbled off and hurried away.

By the early 1990s, I had spent 10 years studying bears and had written three books about these impressive carnivores. On my first trip to Antarctica, many people assumed I was going there to continue my study of bears. Of course, there are no bears in Antarctica or anywhere else penguins live. I went to Antarctica simply to see how it compared with the Arctic, and unexpectedly, I fell in love. Penguin colonies were like nothing I had ever seen — so much activity, so much noise, so many odors, so much life. Perhaps it was the penguins' unwary nature, their familiar upright stance or their comical waddle that won my heart. It didn't really matter why I found penguins interesting — I was hooked.

My search for penguins has taken me over 400,000 miles (644 000 km), from the frozen edges of Antarctica and the wave-battered shorelines of New Zealand's Antipodes Islands to the sun-scorched beaches of the Galápagos Islands and the rugged coast of Chile's Atacama Desert. For me penguins have become more than cute birds that waddle and bray; they are exciting creatures with lives as complicated as our own. In *Penguins!* I will share with you the exciting details of how these flightless seabirds thrive in their world. It is not only a wonderful story of scientific discovery but also one filled with surprises and tantalizing secrets.

Penguins occupy a surprising range of habitats: the heathlands of Campbell Island, New Zealand; ice-choked Antarctica; equatorial Bartolomé Island, the Galápagos Islands; and the temperate rainforests of South Island, New Zealand.

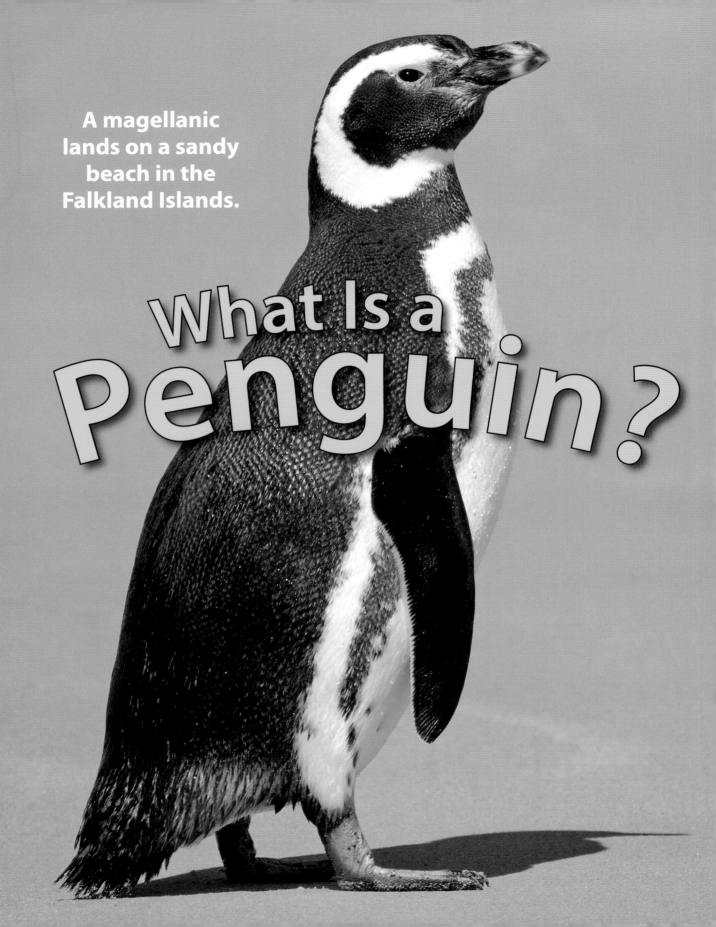

A magellanic lands on a sandy beach in the Falkland Islands.

What Is a Penguin?

The first Europeans to see penguins were the sailors in wooden ships that creaked and pitched around the southern capes of Africa and South America about 500 years ago. The grizzled seafarers who weathered those storm-battered waters couldn't decide whether penguins were mammals, birds or fish, so they settled on "feathered fish." They were half right. Penguins are covered with feathers, but they are definitely birds — flightless seabirds. Today everyone agrees there are at least 18 different kinds of these "feathered fish," although the number may soon increase to 20. Recent genetic studies strongly suggest that the little penguin of Australia and New Zealand may actually represent two separate species. And the feisty southern rockhopper penguin probably also represents two different species, a western one in the southern Atlantic Ocean and an eastern one in the southern Indian and Pacific Oceans. These latest discoveries are compelling, and throughout the book, I will treat the penguin family as if it now has 20 members rather than 18.

The Maori natives of New Zealand have an old legend about how the first penguin became flightless. Back in the distant past, a penguin named Tawaki and an albatross named Taroa argued continually about which of them was better at fishing and flying. The constant bickering annoyed Tāne Mahuta, the god of the forests and birds, and he took the two birds aside and gave each a special skill. To Taroa he gave the longest wings of any seabird so that the albatross could soar far from land on the ocean winds, in search of food. To Tawaki he gave powerful flippers so that the penguin could fly beneath the ocean waves to catch all the fish it would ever need.

Paleontologists, scientists who study fossils, offer an even better explanation about how the penguin lost its wings. The earliest penguins were comparatively small flying seabirds, no bigger than the present-day puffin. Like puffins, these earliest penguins used their wings to swim underwater *and* to fly in the air. Since water is much denser than air, no wing can work equally well in both. The reasons for this are simple. In air, a bird's wings provide lift as well as forward motion, and they need a relatively large surface area to accomplish this — in short, the wings function like sails. In water, on the other hand, most birds are neutrally buoyant, so they don't need their wings for lift, only for forward motion. The best underwater

Penguin Relatives

Penguins were not always flightless. Researchers now believe that penguins evolved from a group of flying seabirds called "tubenoses," so named because their nostrils are located at the end of a tube on the top of their beak. Today the tubenoses include albatrosses and petrels, some of the greatest fliers in the world. According to scientists, the earliest penguins branched off from the tubenose group around 70 million years ago, shortly before the dinosaurs disappeared.

The wandering albatross has a wingspan up to 11.5 feet (3.5 m), the longest of any bird.

wings act like paddles and have a relatively small surface area. Early in their evolution, penguins gave up flying in favor of improved underwater swimming. Their wings became modified into little, stiff flippers that could propel the penguins underwater faster and deeper than any other bird. The flightless penguins had arrived.

Once penguins no longer needed their wings for flight, they could get much bigger — and they did just that. Today the largest penguin alive is the emperor, which stands over 3 feet tall (90 cm) and can weigh 88 pounds (40 kg) or more. The heaviest emperor on record weighed 101 pounds (46 kg), which is heavier than some female gymnasts at the last summer Olympics. Among the early penguins, nearly half of them were larger than the emperor is today, and some of them were very much larger. The largest penguin ever discovered, the now-extinct *Palaeeudyptes klekowskii,* has no common name, but if ever I met one in a dark alley, I would call it "sir." The burly *Palaeeudyptes* stood as tall as 5 feet (150 cm) and weighed nearly 254 pounds (115 kg).

For many millions of years, penguins were the main warm-blooded predators of fish, squid and krill in the southern oceans of the world. When the dinosaurs became extinct, many marine reptiles also disappeared, and penguins simply took their place. The reign of the penguin clan lasted for perhaps 15 to 20 million years, during which time there were as many as 40 different kinds of these flipper-powered predators roving the seas. Then, roughly 25 million years ago, the small toothed whales, seals and sea lions arrived on the scene and everything changed. Suddenly, the penguins, especially the large species, were faced with some fast-swimming competition, and the penguins lost. When the sea spray settled, only the smaller penguins had survived. Those are the species we have with us today.

Meet the Family

In 1914 British Antarctic explorer George Murray Levick wrote about one of the penguins in this way:

> Imagine a little man, standing erect, provided with two broad paddles instead of arms, with a head small in comparison with the plump stout body; imagine this creature with his back covered with a black coat ... tapering behind to a pointed tail that drags on the ground, and adorned in front with a glossy white breast-plate. Have this creature walk on his two feet, and give him at the same time a droll little waddle, and a pert movement of the head; you have before you something irresistibly attractive and comical.

The black wingtips on an Adélie contain melanin, a beneficial pigment that resists wear and strengthens the feathers.

11

The head feathers on the crested penguins vary slightly in color, length and shape, as seen in the royal *(left)*, southern rockhopper *(below right)* and macaroni *(below left)*.

Levick was describing an Adélie penguin, the species commonly pictured in advertising and the one most people think of as the typical penguin. Today, however, most scientists recognize 20 different kinds of penguins, which are divided into six groups.

The largest group of penguins in the family includes the eight crested species: royal, macaroni, northern rockhopper, southern rockhopper, eastern rockhopper, erect-crested, fiordland and snares. All of them have wispy yellow or orange head plumes, and a feisty disposition to match their wild hairdos. The medium-sized crested penguins stand roughly 2 feet tall (60 cm) and weigh anywhere from 5 to 18 pounds (2.25–8 kg). One of the largest crested species, the macaroni penguin, is the most numerous penguin of all, boasting over six million pairs. In fact, nearly a third of all the penguins in the world are macaronis.

The four banded penguins (magellanic, Humboldt, African and Galápagos species) compose a second group. They are sometimes called "jackass penguins," because all of them bray like donkeys. When a whole colony of these loudmouths begins to holler, the racket can be deafening. All the banded penguins have either a single or a double black band across their upper chest and are small to medium in size, weighing between 4 and 14 pounds (2–6.5 kg). Among the banded penguins, two species — the Galápagos and the African — are currently endangered, as both have small, vulnerable breeding populations. The Galápagos, numbering fewer than

The facial feathering and chest bands differ among the four banded penguins: Galápagos *(top left)*, magellanic *(top right)*, African *(bottom left)* and Humboldt *(bottom right)*.

2,000 adults, is the rarest of all penguins and could face extinction in this century.

A third group of penguins is the three brush-tailed penguins, which includes the familiar tuxedo-clad Adélie, the chinstrap and the gentoo. The chinstrap, like the Adélie, is a plain black-and-white penguin, with pudgy pink feet. The gentoo, by comparison, is the most colorful of the three, with a bright orange beak and a matching set of color-coordinated feet. Members of the brush-tailed trio are medium in size, weighing between 7 and 14 pounds (3–6.5 kg), and all have a longer-

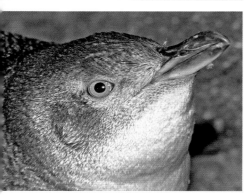

than-usual tail of stiff quills, from which the group derives its name.

The two largest penguins, the king and the emperor, make up a fourth group. Their large size — an average 33 pounds (15 kg) in kings and 77 pounds (35 kg) in emperors — enables them to perform feats of endurance beyond the capability of the smaller species. The king and the emperor dive the deepest, withstand the coldest winter temperatures and travel the farthest on feeding trips of any of the penguin species.

The fifth group of penguins contains two species: the little penguin of Australia and the recently recognized white-flippered penguin of New Zealand. These are the smallest members of the penguin family, weighing less than 3 pounds (1.5 kg) soaking wet.

The sixth and final group consists of just one species: the yellow-eyed penguin. When compared with the tiny little

Top: The long tail on the three brush-tailed penguins (left to right Gentoo, Adélie, chinstrap) increases their underwater maneuverability.

Left: The color of a penguin's eyes, yellow in the yellow-eyed and blue-gray in the little penguin, has no influence on the bird's vision and is solely for display.

Top: An adult emperor weighs up to 101 pounds (46 kg).

Bottom: The brightness of the orange ear patch on the king penguin is an important signal of good health.

penguin, the yellow-eyed is a real bruiser and can be six times heavier. Unfortunately, size is no guarantee of survival, and the yellow-eyed penguin, which lives in New Zealand, is highly endangered. Fewer than 5,000 mature adults remain.

It is one thing to divide the penguin family into six tidy groups and quite another to identify which bird is which. Body size is a good place to start, since each species generally falls into a single category: small, medium or large. Beyond that, plumage pattern is the main key to penguin identification. All 20 species have roughly the same body coloration: dark gray or black on the back, with a bright white chest and belly. This common color pattern has led naturalists to joke that there are really just two kinds of penguins: the black ones running away from you and the white ones coming toward you.

When a penguin is floating quietly on the surface of the water, only its head and neck are visible. Luckily, these parts of the bird carry many identifying characteristics: differences in the size and color of the bill; the presence or absence of a bright, conspicuous crest; and distinctive patterns of color on the head and neck. Penguins likely rely on the appearance of these body parts to identify one another. Human birdwatchers use these same clues to distinguish the different species.

Penguin Places

When most people think of penguins, they think of Antarctica, icebergs and numbing cold; of tough birds beaten by blizzards, huddling over their nests on frigid sea ice or bare rock. Although two species — Adélie and emperor — live like this, most penguins live where conditions are much different.

How many species?

Worldwide, there are roughly 10,000 species of birds. Obviously, the 20 species in the penguin family represent a very small proportion of these. Yet for such a small family of flightless birds, penguins have managed to occupy a greater range of latitudes and temperatures than almost any other avian family on Earth

The beak on the snares penguin is one of the largest among the eight crested penguins.

Penguins evolved in the Southern Hemisphere, probably in the cool ocean waters between 50 and 55 degrees south latitude. Today these same waters south of New Zealand are home to nine different species of penguins, a greater variety than anywhere else on Earth. But the early penguins had wanderlust, and they gradually paddled their way into other areas of the ocean north and south, until they finally ranged from the icy shores of Antarctica to the searing lava rocks of the equator. Today penguins live with koalas in southern Australia and parrots in New Zealand. In southern Africa they make their homes alongside leopards and hyenas, and in the Galápagos Islands the local penguins share the shoreline with marine iguanas. Clearly, penguins are extremely adaptable birds.

Oceans cover roughly 80 percent of the Southern Hemisphere, and you might expect an adaptable seabird such as the penguin to live wherever there is salt water. Not so. Penguins are not evenly distributed over the vast oceans of the hemisphere. Ocean areas differ greatly in the amount of plankton they produce. A number are particularly rich and have therefore attracted the greatest numbers of penguins. Predictably, penguins are at home where the fish are jumpin' and the livin' is easy. Wherever cold, oxygen-charged water, rich in nutrients, mixes and wells to the surface, plankton multiply, and the fish, krill and penguins follow. Such areas occur along the southwestern coastlines of South America and Africa, where they are named the Humboldt and Benguela Currents respectively. Three species of penguins are nourished by these fertile, cold coastal currents.

The Antarctic Convergence is another rich ocean area where penguins concentrate. Here, the cold, dense waters of the Southern Ocean, which surrounds Antarctica, meet and dip beneath the warm, saltier waters of the southern Atlantic, Indian and Pacific Oceans. The mixing of the different waters creates ideal conditions for the growth of plankton, and penguins profit as a result.

With so many penguins thriving in the cold waters of the Southern Hemisphere, why are there none in the Northern Hemisphere? A major barrier to the migration of penguins north is the warm waters of the tropics, which are relatively poor in dissolved oxygen and nutrients. In such waters, penguins would have trouble finding enough food to fuel them on their long journey north. Thus, thousands of miles separate most penguin populations in the south from the cold, rich northern waters of the Atlantic and Pacific. Penguins *could* live in the cold waters of the Northern Hemisphere — if only they could get there.

During the 1930s, Norwegian whalers transported and released off the northern coast of Norway several dozen king penguins,

Top to bottom: Royal penguins, Australia's Macquarie Island; emperor penguins, Weddell Sea, Antarctica; yellow-eyed penguin, New Zealand's Enderby Island.

Rich "upwellings" of cold water that is rich in nutrients occur in South America, Africa, the Antarctic Peninsula and along the coastlines of several dozen island clusters scattered around the entire perimeter of the continent. Islands such as South Georgia, the South Sandwiches, Kerguelens, Crozets and Macquarie are world renowned for their huge penguin colonies.

Where Penguins Are Found

Adélie penguins nest the farthest south in Antarctica of any species of penguin.

chinstraps and macaronis. Some of the transplanted penguins lived for more than 10 years, but none of them ever bred, and all of them eventually disappeared.

Hot and Cold Penguins

The body temperature of an emperor penguin huddled in a winter blizzard on Antarctica at minus 40 degrees F (−40°C) is the same as that of a Humboldt penguin loafing on the coastline of the Atacama Desert in Chile at 108 degrees F (42°C). There is, however, one big difference. The emperor must conserve body heat to keep from freezing to death, and the Humboldt must shed body heat to avoid being cooked alive. The penguin family has evolved a fascinating series of adaptations to deal with such temperature extremes.

A thick layer of feathers helps all birds stay warm. Penguins have carried this adaptation a step further. A penguin's body feathers are surprisingly small for the size of the bird. Most of the feathers are lance shaped, with a stiff vein down the center and a small tuft of down at the base. Because of their design, the feathers overlap like roof tiles and are not easily ruffled in strong winds that can rob a penguin of body heat. The tufts of down add further insulation by trapping a layer of warm air next to the bird's skin.

King penguins *(above left)* live in warmer areas than emperors *(above right)* and need less feathering on their legs.

The penguin has two other aces up its flipper. First, a penguin's body is covered with feathers; the feathers on most other birds are arranged in tracts, with bare spaces in between. You can discover this for yourself by examining the pattern of small bumps on the skin of a roast turkey or chicken. The bumps are feather follicles. Notice how they are clustered on the skin and how some areas of the skin have no follicles at all. The complete feather covering on a penguin provides better insulation than if the feathers were arranged in tracts. Second, every square inch of a penguin's body has up to 80 feathers packed into it, three to four times more feathers than in any other group of seabirds.

It is not enough for some penguins simply to conserve body heat with a thick covering of feathers. They must also be protected against excessive heat loss from their beaks, flippers and legs. A comparison between the polar emperor penguin and its close relative, the king, which lives in a warmer climate, will illustrate how some penguins beat the chill. Even though emperors are twice as heavy as king penguins, they have a shorter beak, shorter flippers and smaller feet. These adaptations all reduce the loss of body heat. Furthermore, the legs on an emperor penguin are covered with feathers and only its toes are bare, while the toes *and* legs of the king penguin are bare.

Flipper and beak adjustments can occur, as well, within a single species of penguin that lives in a wide range of climates. For example, gentoo penguins nesting at 65 degrees south latitude on Pleneau Island, along the Antarctic Peninsula, have shorter beaks and flippers than gentoos nesting 900 miles (1,450 km) farther north, on the relatively warm Falkland Islands.

When they can't shorten their beaks any further, some penguins use another heat-saving device: feathers. This adaptation is best illustrated in the three closely related members of the brush-tailed penguin group. The gentoo penguin, which generally nests in the warmest conditions of the three, has no feathers insulating its beak. The

Penguins living in cold climates have more feathers covering their beak than their warm-weather relatives. Compare the three brushtails above: chinstrap *(left)*, Adelie *(center)* and gentoo *(right)*, and two of the banded group, the Humboldt *(right)* and magellanic *(far right)*.

chinstrap, which nests in colder climates, has feathers covering the inner third of its beak. The Adélie, which nests farther south than any penguin — 77 degrees south latitude — has half its beaked wrapped in fine feathers. Or a penguin can cut heat loss through its beak by tucking it under a warm flipper when sleeping.

You might think that penguins could also rely on their fat to insulate them against the cold waters in which they swim, but this is not the case. Scientists now believe that penguins use their fat mainly as an energy reserve and not as a heating blanket. In fact, when some of the large penguins, such as kings and emperors, dive, they *need* to lose body heat to stay underwater longer. I will talk more about this exciting new discovery later.

The final way in which penguins can stay warm is to huddle. Once they reach the age of a month or so, the chicks of many penguin species clump together when the weather gets bad and share body heat. However, the real test of huddling as a heat saver is seen with the adult emperor penguin. In this species, each male must incubate a single egg through the worst of the Antarctic winter. With some large emperor colonies, several thousand adult males may huddle up, eight birds per square yard (10/sq m), to withstand the numbing cold and winds of a blizzard.

Since an incubating male emperor may need to fast, stretching his fat reserves for up to three months, he needs to save as much energy as he can. Without these huddles, a male emperor could never fast this long, and he would have no choice but to abandon his egg and head back to sea.

Because penguins evolved in a cool oceanic environment, it's no surprise that

The temperature inside emperor penguin huddles may be 18 Fahrenheit degrees (10C°) warmer than the outside air, and this means energy savings for the huddlers. Emperors outside a huddle lose twice as much weight as those crammed into the crowd.

Huddling for Survival

they're well adapted to keeping warm. But how do the well-insulated birds cool off? Every penguin builds up body heat when it is swimming, even in the coldest water, so all penguins require some way to get rid of excess heat. One way is to send blood to their flippers. The feathers on a penguin's flippers are small and scale-like and have very little insulation. Warm blood diverted to the flippers is therefore quickly cooled by the surrounding water or air. When a penguin first lands on shore, its flippers are often flushed pink with blood; the bird holds them out from its side to allow the air to cool them.

The greatest adaptations to overheating are found in the banded penguins, the species that live in the warmest climates. As I mentioned earlier, a penguin loses body heat through its beak, but it can also lose heat through the skin on its face. The faces of all the cold-climate penguins are covered with feathers, but not so the

warm-weather species. Magellanic and African penguins, have bare, featherless skin between their eyes and at the base of their beaks. In the Humboldt and Galápagos penguins, the bare area is larger and extends beyond the beak. When these birds build up too much body heat, they simply divert more blood to the skin of their face to cool off. Humans do something very similar. After a long run, a jogger's face is as red as a radish.

Top: Adélie chicks huddle for warmth in the cold.

Left: Penguins have the thickest feathers of all the seabirds, and if penguins get overheated, they need to lose body heat through their feet, beak and wings.

A gentoo runs as fast as it can when it first comes ashore.

Penguins in Motion

P enguins spend most of their lives at sea. Some species may not even touch land for six or seven months at a stretch. Fiordland penguins, belonging to the crested group, may spend so much time riding the swell off the coast of New Zealand that barnacles begin to grow on their tail feathers. Clearly, penguins are most at home in the water, and if there is one thing they do well, swimming is it.

A penguin may never win a beauty contest for its curves and hourglass figure, but it has the perfect torpedo shape to slice through the water. When a penguin is swimming underwater, its head is tucked snugly between its shoulders and its feet trail behind, making the bird as streamlined as possible. The fastest penguin swimmers are the large species — the kings and the emperors. A flipper-powered emperor can torpedo through the water at up to 18 miles an hour (29 km/h), more than three times as fast as an Olympic swimmer.

Adélies, and most other penguins, travel in groups when they are near shore, to protect themselves from predators.

Outmaneuvering Predators

Penguins need maneuverability not only to catch their fast-swimming prey but also to escape from predators. Under most circumstances, sharks can fin faster than penguins, and sea lions and fur seals can sprint as fast as an emperor penguin. Remarkably, bull killer whales can accelerate to 34 miles an hour (55 km/h). It's quite clear that without their maneuverability most pursued penguins would soon be dead penguins.

Maneuverability is just as important as speed, and a penguin is particularly agile underwater. In one study, a Humboldt penguin proved that it could completely reverse its direction while traveling just a quarter of its body length, a mere 6 inches (15 cm). The penguin could achieve this remarkable feat even when it was swimming at maximum speed. A penguin uses its feet, tail and laterally flattened beak as steering devices, and all three in combination is what gives this bird such extraordinary underwater agility.

Porpoising is another tactic that many penguins use to keep from becoming somebody's dinner. In porpoising, a penguin combines underwater sprints with low-level aerial leaps. This method of travel confuses underwater predators. When a penguin arcs out of the water, it is momentarily lost from view to a pursuer. Once the bird dives in again, it often makes a sudden change in its direction of travel. This surprises a predator and gains the penguin a brief advantage. After this happens a few times, the predator frequently abandons the chase.

Top: An Adélie comes ashore.
Right: A porpoising gentoo.

Dive, Dive, Dive

Although penguins are accomplished swimmers, diving is what they do better than any other seabird. Most penguin species can reach depths of 300 feet (91 m) and stay submerged for five or six minutes. More commonly, however, they stay underwater for just a minute or two and dive no deeper than 150 feet (50 m).

All the deep divers, including penguins, breathe air. To remain submerged, deep divers must bring extra oxygen with them, stored in their lungs, blood and muscles. When scientists analyzed the extra oxygen in the lungs, air sacs, blood and muscles of kings and emperor penguins, they were puzzled. There simply was not enough oxygen for the birds to stay submerged as long as they did. Recent research may have finally solved the mystery.

Deep-diving penguins chill out. During a deep dive, a king penguin allows the

King penguins dive deeper than all penguins except emperors.

Diving Records

Not surprisingly, the diving records are held by the largest penguins, the kings and the emperors. Kings have been recorded at depths of 1,060 feet (325 m) and big-bodied emperors can plunge to 1,850 feet (564 m) and stay submerged for nearly 28 minutes. Just for comparison, the depth record held by a human free diver is 420 feet (128 m), and the diver held his breath for just four minutes and 10 seconds. Other deep divers include leatherback turtles, the largest living sea turtle, which hunt jellyfish to depths of 3,900 feet (1 190 m), and bull sperm whales, which stalk bottom-dwelling sharks 10,000 feet (3 050 m) down. Remarkably, a hunting sperm whale may stay submerged for nearly two hours!

A king penguin may make over 600 dives on a fishing trip.

Penguin Mysteries

Human pearl divers in the South Pacific — many of them only 12 or 13 years old — make 40 to 60 dives in a day. But sometimes the young divers suffer decompression sickness and become paralyzed or die from it. When a pearl diver makes multiple dives and does not spend enough time at the surface between dives, nitrogen accumulates in the blood, and when it reaches a certain level, bubbles form in the bloodstream. These bubbles cause the greatest damage when they block tiny blood vessels inside the brain. In theory, diving penguins should also suffer from decompression sickness. How they avoid this is yet another mystery that surrounds the lives of these fascinating flightless seabirds.

An iceberg makes a safe resting spot for an Adélie.

cold water in which it is swimming to drain heat from its body so that the temperature inside its abdomen drops from a normal 102 degrees F (39°C) to an unbelievable 52 degrees F (11°C). Chilling its body core reduces the amount of oxygen the penguin burns. As a result, the extra oxygen it stores in its lungs, air sacs, blood and muscles lasts longer and the penguin can stay underwater for a greater length of time. Exciting discoveries like these are the reason I find animal behavior so rewarding to study, and they have fueled my lifelong passion for science.

Not only is a penguin able to dive deeply but it is also able to do it over and over again. On a typical feeding trip, a penguin may make a remarkable number of dives. A king penguin searching for lanternfish may dive 144 times in a day, and a krill-catching macaroni may go under 244 times in only 12 hours. As far as I know, the record number of dives is held by a gentoo penguin, which made 460 dives in just 15 hours! That's roughly one dive every two minutes.

Back on the Beach

In water, a penguin can change direction in a heartbeat, rocket six feet (2 m) into the air to reach the safety of an iceberg and dive to crushing depths. On land, however, the penguin turns competence into comedy as it waddles, hops and toboggans. A penguin's legs are as far back on its body as they can be without falling off. In this position, legs are ideal as an underwater rudder, but it's a different story when their owner hits the shore. You might say a penguin on land sways more than walks, rocking from side to side like an old sailor home from the sea. And the fatter the penguin is, the more it sways.

I once laughed as a plumped-up king penguin came ashore. The bird could

Slipping and Sliding

Tobogganing on their bellies saves the penguins considerable energy, and if several of them follow each other beak to tail, the bellies of those in the lead can wear a groove in the snow and make the going that much easier for those in the rear.

A tobogganing emperor may slide over 60 miles (100 km) on its belly.

Right: A group of kings lands on a colony beach.

Bottom: Like all penguins, gentoos waddle when they walk.

barely stand. As soon as it took a few steps forward, it would lose its balance and topple onto its belly, ramming its beak into the wet sand. The tuckered-out king finally gave up and fell asleep on the beach. Perhaps a few days of dieting would make life easier!

In early spring, an Adélie penguin may need to walk 60 miles (95 km) or more over rough sea ice to reach its nesting colony on the shore. An emperor may face a trek of 120 miles (195 km) in a similar goal. For both penguins, that's a long way to waddle and sway. Emperors and Adélies have devised a method to lessen the labor of such a journey: they lie down on the job and toboggan. After flopping onto their bellies, they slide forward using their flippers for balance and the long claws on their toes for traction.

Another way a penguin gets around on land is by hopping, and the three well-named rockhoppers do this better than all others. Seabird specialist Robert Cushman Murphy wrote, "Picture a penguin with a yellow pompon over each eye, and a gait that caused the early visitors to the Falklands to dub it the 'Jumping Jack.' Instead of walking, it progresses in a series of bounds executed with an elasticity of motion such as is exhibited by a kangaroo." The rockhoppers, the smallest of the eight crested penguins, may not have size, but they certainly have perseverance. Some rockhoppers may climb 500 feet (150 m) up rocky cliffs and steep slopes to reach their nesting colony, making the difficult trip one six-inch (15 cm) hop at a time. On the Steeple Jason Islands, in the Falklands, the claws of countless climbing rockhoppers have scratched deep grooves into the rocks.

When gentoos eat krill, it colors their droppings — and the snow in their colony — pink.

What's on the Menu?

Penguins, like most seabirds, are strictly meat eaters, and their diet consists of just three kinds of seafood: fish, squid and crustaceans, including krill, a shrimp look-alike. Even so, their menu is more varied than it might seem. For example, little penguins in Australia eat 28 different fish, and some African penguins dine on 18 kinds of crustaceans and 25 different fish. In the past there was only one way for a scientist to learn what a penguin had eaten: kill the bird and examine the contents of its stomach. Nowadays a researcher simply catches the penguin, threads a hollow tube down its throat and flushes out the bird's stomach. As a former emergency room doctor, I did this same thing many times to patients who had taken drug overdoses. Certainly, no one ever enjoyed the procedure, but it caused folks no harm. I expect that penguins are no different. Flushing a penguin's stomach steals a meal from the bird but causes no physical injury, although the psychological trauma of being restrained by a fuzzy-faced scientist having a bad hair day may motivate the bird to steer clear of humans forever afterward.

Once researchers flush the slimy stomach soup from a penguin, how do they sort out the goo? Luckily, the outer skeletons of most crustaceans are made of chitin, a stiff, tough material that is hard to digest. As a result, a crustacean can be identified long after it has been eaten. Identifying fish and squid is even easier. The scales of fish and the inner ear bones of squid, called "otoliths," are composed of dense calcium, so they are likewise very resistant to digestion and can be used for identification many days after a meal is swallowed. Squid provide yet another clue to their identity. The sharp, horny beak that squid use to bite and kill their prey is unaffected by penguin stomach acid, so the size of the beak can also be used to estimate the squid's body size. From this

The yellow staining on this chinstrap *(top)* indicates a diet of squid, and the white droppings on the gentoo *(bottom)* are from a diet of fish.

Penguins are mainly daytime hunters, feeding during the middle hours of the day when the sun is highest in the sky. At this time the light penetrates deepest into the water.

Daytime Eaters

Gentoos often leave for fishing trips early in the morning.

scientists have determined that emperor penguins sometimes tackle squid 2 feet (60 cm) long.

I've watched thousands of penguins but have never flushed a penguin's stomach. Even so, there is another way to discover what a penguin has been eating, and that is to examine the goo *after* it leaves the penguin. The color of penguin droppings, called "guano," varies as the bird's diet changes. A diet of fish produces white or gray droppings. Krill, a shrimp-like crustacean, yields pink poop, and penguin-processed squid is yellow. A penguin that has been fasting for more than a few days has green, bile-stained guano. Streaks of colored guano radiate from the edges of most penguin nests. You probably wouldn't think of calling a penguin an artist unless you'd seen the bird pucker and let the guano fly. Explorer and author Murray Levick, who may have spent a little too much time pondering penguin poop, wrote, "The excreta of Adélies ... are squirted clear of the [nests] for a distance of a foot or more so that each nest has the appearance of a flower with bright green petals radiating from its center."

In the Falkland Islands I learned that the splatter zone extends to the nest of a neighbor. Even so, the birds do not seem too disturbed when they get pasted. One southern rockhopper I watched was within range when its neighbor let the guano go.

The rockhopper took a full shot in the face. The plastered penguin simply shook its head, snorted and allowed the wet goo to slowly drip from its beak and golden crest.

The color of guano can signal a sudden change in a penguin's diet. On a recent trip to Antarctica I visited a colony of chinstrap penguins on the island of South Georgia. The birds were filthy and badly soiled with dried guano of two different colors: fresh pink plastered over white. Clearly, the diet of the chinstraps had changed in a matter of weeks, from fish earlier in the season to krill.

Chasing the Chow

While it's interesting to know what penguins eat, it is even more interesting to learn how they catch their food. When penguins leave a colony on a feeding trip, they commonly travel in groups of 10 to 30 birds. However, once they reach the area they want to search, they often split into singles, pairs and trios. But even when three or four penguins remain together, they seem to hunt as individuals and do not cooperate in locating or catching prey, as do killer whales and some birds of prey among others.

Penguins are visual hunters and rely primarily on their eyesight to find food. Their eyes are not particularly large, nor do they have any special reflective layers behind the retinas to amplify the light, as do many nocturnal animals.

In most oceans sunlight usually never reaches deeper than 650 feet (200 m), yet

A group of macaroni penguins finds a school of fish easier than a macaroni hunting alone.

as we have seen, king and emperor penguins dive well beyond these depths. How do these deep divers find their prey in the total darkness? The answer is bioluminescence. Many squid and crustaceans and some of the fish that penguins hunt have luminous spots scattered over their bodies. These spots flash and glow in the dark, and penguins probably use them to locate their prey.

Most of the prey that penguins hunt occur in clumps containing many individuals. Schools of anchovies, for example, may contain thousands of these small fish, and swarms of krill sometimes number in the millions. Immense "super swarms" of krill may redden the surface of the ocean for 50 square miles (130 sq km) and extend 325 feet (100 m) down. If you were to dip a water pitcher into such a dense swarm, you would catch hundreds of krill. Multiply that by tens of millions, and you have some idea how many krill there are in such a swarm.

The challenge for a penguin is to locate the swarms and schools scattered over the vastness of the ocean. As a result, a hunting penguin may search a long time before it finally finds food, but when it does, it is a skilled predator. Banded penguins that prey mainly on schools of fish have a special technique for catching their

The inside of a southern rockhopper's mouth is a fish trap.

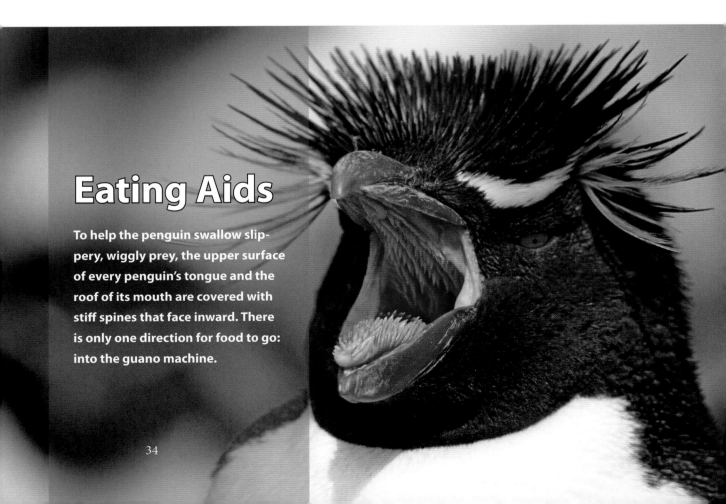

Eating Aids

To help the penguin swallow slippery, wiggly prey, the upper surface of every penguin's tongue and the roof of its mouth are covered with stiff spines that face inward. There is only one direction for food to go: into the guano machine.

34

The hooked tip on a Galápagos penguin's beak improves its grip on wriggling prey.

quarry. All four species of banded penguins have black-and-white stripes on their flanks, and this bold pattern may startle the fish when the birds circle them. A penguin's tactic is to circle a school repeatedly and bunch the fish tighter and tighter. Eventually, the fish get packed so tightly that the coordination of the school breaks down. When this happens, the fish get confused and flee in all directions. And that's when the penguin strikes. After diving beneath the school, it swims through it from below, grabbing the frightened fish one after another. The dark plumage of a penguin's back when seen from above against the depths of the ocean hides the bird's approach until it is too late for the prey to react.

Penguins catch their prey one at a time. If the prey is small, they swallow it underwater and continue fishing. In this way a gentoo may capture 100 krill in a single dive, and a king penguin may nab 29 lanternfish before it returns to the surface to breathe.

Not everything a penguin swallows wiggles and squirms. Sometimes penguins eat rocks. I once followed a parade of chinstraps as they waddled from their nesting colony back to the ocean. Along the way two of the birds each picked up a small

An Appetite for Rocks

It was a penguin's appetite for pebbles that suggested the existence of Antarctica before the continent was discovered. In 1840 an American expedition captured an emperor penguin at 66 degrees 52 minutes south latitude, just inside the Antarctic Circle. When the penguin's stomach was dissected, the sailors were surprised to find pebbles of basalt, a volcanic rock. They reasoned that the bird must have traveled from some unknown land. They were right.

Emperor penguins nest around the entire edge of Antarctica.

pebble from the path and carried it in its beak. When the penguins finally disappeared into the surf, each still had the pebble clamped in its mouth. Many species of penguins have stones in their stomachs; a large emperor may carry a pound (450 g) of them.

The whalers and sealers of the 1800s were convinced that penguins swallowed stones to help them control their buoyancy, but modern scientists still have no satisfactory explanation for this behavior.

Feeding the Kids

Scientists estimate that on an average day, a penguin will stuff itself with seafood amounting to about 20 percent of its own body weight. I weigh 180 pounds (82 kg), and if I did the same, I would need to gobble and gulp my way through 36 pounds (16 kg) of food. Surprisingly, a penguin may stuff itself even more when it has a chick to feed. In such cases some Adélies may load up with 40,000 krill. A magellanic penguin in Argentina was caught with 22 squid in its gut. The squid weighed a belly-bursting nine pounds (4 kg), nearly the same weight as the bird itself.

A penguin chick rarely needs urging to eat. As soon as a parent returns to the

An emperor chick vibrates its beak against the beak of its parent if it wants to be fed.

An Adélie chick may chase its parent for five minutes before it finally gets a meal.

nest, a chick starts to chirp. The young bird stimulates the adults to feed it by rapidly vibrating its beak against that of its parent. When the adult bird opens its mouth, the chick wedges its bill inside and gobbles up the slimy goo. The head of a small chick may disappear completely inside a parent's throat. Typically, a chick receives eight to 12 servings like this, until the parent bird has nothing left to regurgitate. A large, well-fed chinstrap chick may receive 1.5 pounds (680 g) in a single meal, and a king penguin chick may gobble down 6.5 pounds (3 kg) — so much food that the chick looks like an overstuffed laundry bag.

Mealtime for chicks is not always so orderly. The brush-tailed penguins, for

Sometimes a hungry gentoo chick can't wait for its parent to reach the shore before being fed.

example, commonly have two chicks in a family, and in these species *mealtime* is just another word for *food fight*. When the chicks are small, the bigger of the two simply bullies its sibling and steals most of the chow. After a month or so the hungry chicks must run for their dinner. I watched these "feeding chases," as they are called, in gentoo penguins many times in the Falkland Islands, and this is how I described the action in my journal:

> Suddenly, the chase is on, and the adult bird appears to be running for its life, closely followed by two imploring chicks. The eagerness of the chicks can be so great that they run into the rear of the adult, stepping on its tail. I sometimes wonder whether the chicks might not keep on running right up their parent's back if the adult stopped without warning.
>
> The dogged chicks shadow the parent's every dodge and turn and are remarkably fast despite their potbellied profiles. As they run along, they chirp loudly and flap their flippers limply. A chase often lasts a minute or two, with the penguins cutting through the colony in a zigzag course, along one edge and then back through the crowd again. Invariably, one of the chicks tires and drops out of the race. Shortly after that, the adult stops and allows the remaining runner to catch up if it has lagged behind ... Soon a slimy wad of regurgitated fish slides down the parent's beak into the gape of the chick — the reward for perseverance.

The Mating Game

Most southern rockhoppers mate with the same partner they had the previous year.

The mating season is one of the most important yearly events in a penguin's life. For most species the season starts in September and October, the spring months in the Southern Hemisphere. The activity begins when the birds, fat and full of fight, gather in crowded colonies to strut their stuff.

Penguin colonies come in three sizes: small, large, and beyond belief. Almost every species has its share of small colonies, where one or two dozen pairs cluster. In some cases these are satellite colonies that were established when larger colonies became overpopulated. Large colonies are common among penguins. Consider the 25,000 pairs of northern rockhoppers in a single colony on Tristan da Cunha, or the 50,000 pairs of kings at Lusitania Bay on Macquarie Island. Such a concentration of bird life is truly breathtaking to witness.

Unbelievably, some penguins live life on an even larger scale: 270,000 pairs of Adélies crowd the slopes of Cape Adare on the ice-choked coast of Antarctica;

A chinstrap colony in Antarctica may be hundreds of years old.

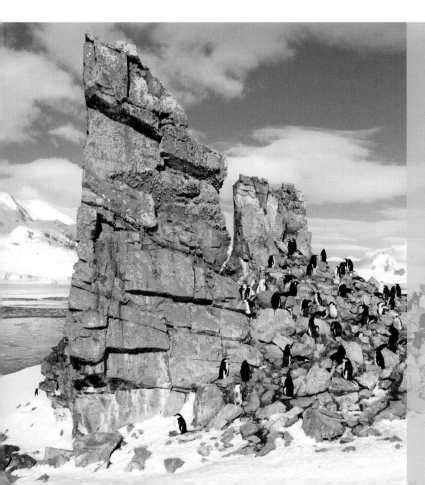

Ancient Graveyards

Penguin colonies can be very old. Bird artist Roger Tory Peterson called them "ancient graveyards" built on the bones and guano of countless generations of breeding birds. Some Adélie colonies in Antarctica may be several thousand years old, and one macaroni colony on Marion Island has been in use for at least 7,000 years.

41

Gentoos *(left)* usually nest close to their neighbors, whereas the yellow-eyed penguin *(bottom, left)* likes to nest far from its neighbors.

400,000 pairs of macaroni penguins cluster on Possession Island; and an astounding five million pairs of chinstraps crowd and compete on the cinder and ash of the volcanic South Sandwich Islands. In colonies of this size the air pulsates with life. So many beating flippers and hearts, so much noise and odor, so much sex and energy — nothing else on Earth compares with it.

Although penguin colonies differ greatly in size, the spacing between the birds is usually fairly constant for each species, even when there is room for them to spread out. For example, magellanic penguins typically nest in burrows three to four feet (1 m) apart whether there are a few hundred birds or a few thousand. The large crested penguins (macaronis, royals and erect-crested species) pack together much closer, with two to three pairs sharing a square yard. *Sharing* is probably the wrong word, since the bad-tempered birds squabble and fight continually. They actually space themselves just beyond pecking distance of one another. The tightest squeeze occurs with emperor penguins. In a single square yard of colony, eight to 10 big, bulky birds stand shoulder to shoulder. As I noted earlier, these penguins need to share body heat with one another, so they cannot afford to spread out. Instead, emperors are forced to be sociable. At the other end of the scale are the yellow-eyed penguins, the least sociable of the 20 species. Penguins in yellow-eyed colonies, if you could call them colonies at all, nest 50 to 150 yards (45–140 m) apart. Yellow-eyes don't seem to mind *listening* to the neighbors; they just don't want to *see* them. In fact, if two nesting pairs can see each other, one or both of the pairs will often abandon their nest.

The obvious question is "Why are penguins so colony crazy?" To begin with, penguins may crowd together simply because there is a shortage of suitable nesting

A colony of king penguins may contain over 100,000 birds, as does this one on South Georgia Island.

locations. In Antarctica, for example, less than 3 percent of the continent is free of ice and snow during the summer months, so the chinstraps, gentoos and Adélies that nest there have little choice but to cram together. A shortage of space, however, does not explain why most penguins cluster in colonies.

Many seabird biologists think that there are at least four other reasons colonies are so attractive to nesting penguins. First, when penguins nest close together, predators such as gulls and skuas find it harder to land and walk between the nests, as well as to stay outside the pecking range of neighboring penguins.

Another reason to court and breed in colonies is to share information, particularly about the location of food. Swarms of squid, krill and fish are often scattered over the ocean and are therefore difficult to locate. A few penguins searching separately may easily miss such prey. When an entire colony of penguins is hunting over the same area, however, there is a much better chance that at least some of the birds will discover where the food is concentrated. Once they have done so, other members of the colony can follow these birds to the food source.

A third benefit of living in a colony is that it gets the birds into the mating mood. Penguins calling and courting together seem to stimulate one another with their behavior. For example, it is well known that colonial seabirds court and mate more frequently when they are surrounded by neighbors that are also courting. In addition, seabirds in large groups lay their eggs sooner than do those in small

A royal penguin may be nine years old before it finds its first partner.

groups. In short, noisy crowds increase hormone levels in these birds and modify their behavior in a beneficial way.

Finally, in most penguin colonies the majority of chicks hatch at roughly the same time. The sudden arrival of large numbers of young, vulnerable birds saturates the environment of the local predators with potential prey. As a result, the total number of chicks the predators can kill is reduced and the chances that any chick will fall victim are lessened.

Property Problems

A penguin can live a long time — 20 years or more. With such long lives, most penguins do not begin to breed until they are 3 or 4 years old, and some of the large crested species may not breed until they are 8 or 9 years of age. No matter how old they are, though, penguins typically start their love lives in the same colony where they hatched. Young Adélies probably stray the least of any species. Ninety-nine percent of them nest in the same colony where they started life inside an egg, and three-quarters of them within 200 yards (185 m) of where they hatched.

At the beginning of the breeding season, male penguins usually arrive a week or so before the females. Returning to a colony is no guarantee that a penguin will automatically inherit a piece of prime property. The best sites are quickly taken, but often not without a struggle. When the success or failure of breeding is at stake, male penguins are ready to fight.

Penguins are tough birds with thick skin, strong beaks and stiff, bony flippers, and the battles they wage can be surprisingly violent. Many fights are bill-wrestling, chest-bumping, flipper-bashing brawls that end only when both contestants are completely exhausted. The fighters tear at each other with their sharp beaks, and the birds can be left covered in blood. Worse than that, some may be blinded.

I watched a pair of chinstraps battle over the ownership of a prime nest located in the center of a small colony. The warriors beat each other repeatedly with their sturdy flippers as they fought their way across four or five other nesting territories.

44

Having reached the edge of the colony, the penguins continued to thrash and tear at each other across 30 yards (25 m) of gravel beach. The war ended at the water's edge when one of the birds escaped into the surf. The males had battled for nearly five minutes, and the winner's left flipper was dripping with blood. As he waddled back to the colony to claim his prize nest, however, he seemed barely affected by the fight. He had victory to give him strength, and now he was a landowner.

Once a male has won a nest site, the first thing he does is scream about it to the neighbors. The triumphant calls of male penguins are described as trumpeting, braying and coarse wheezing. No matter the word, all are loud and harsh. Often, as soon as one male begins to scream, all the penguins around him also scream — a kind of penguin shouting match that may gradually spread throughout the entire colony. Biologists term these male bragging bouts "ecstatic calls," a way for a male penguin to advertise not only his ownership of a nesting site but also his interest in meeting any female looking for a mate.

A pair of southern rockhoppers preen each other's head feathers to strengthen the bond between them.

Mating Rituals

In the past biologists, most of whom were men, thought that the male penguins did all the choosing and the female simply accepted whichever male showed an interest in her. Today researchers believe that female penguins make the final choice of mate, and they can be very picky. Even when a female joins the same partner she had the previous year, she may still assess his qualities to make sure he is a suitable mate.

45

Left: The trumpeting calls of a king penguin are an important signal to potential partners.

Below: Only one in six emperor penguins will mate with the same partner they did the year before.

Male penguins are not choosy; they will court any female penguin with flippers. Even so, 60 to 90 percent of penguins end up with the same mate they had the previous season. Although penguins rarely mate for life, most macaroni penguins reunite for at least four breeding seasons, and some pairs of yellow-eyes stay with the same mate for up to 13 years.

A female can measure the worth of a male partner in two ways for starters: by his color and by his voice. The bright colors on the head, neck and beak of a penguin can be an indication of the bird's health. A male bird infected with internal parasites, for example, may be weak and unhealthy and the colors on his body dull and washed out. A female penguin with a sharp eye can judge the appearance of the feathers to measure the health and vitality of a potential mate. When inquisitive scientists used shoe polish to blacken the bright orange ear patches on adult male king penguins, the males were unable to attract a mate. Even the other males in the colony ignored the birds and never treated them as rivals.

The female also listens to a potential partner's voice; if it sounds too high, she may look elsewhere for a mate. The tone of a male's ecstatic call is influenced by the size of his body and how much fat he has on it. The call of a fat male with a big body is lower in tone than the call of a slimmer bird. A human cannot hear the difference, but a female penguin certainly can. Big, fat males are attractive because their robust condition indicates that they can forage well and can fast for a long period and incubate the eggs while the female hunts at sea. In the end, female penguins not only look their mates over but also listen closely to their love songs.

Burrows, Nests and Bare Feet

Once a female penguin settles down with a partner, the two begin to build a nest. Penguins live in such a wide range of habitats, from the equator to Antarctica, that it is not surprising the different species build different kinds of nests. The little penguin, white-flippered penguin and the four banded penguins live in the warmest climates. All these species nest in rock crevices, under bushes or in burrows where their eggs and young are shielded from the worst heat of the sun.

Some burrows may be more than 3 feet (90 cm) deep. In the past many banded penguins dug their burrows into the thick layers of guano that had accumulated in the colonies. On the Chincha Islands, off the coast of Peru, for example, the guano was 180 feet (55 m) deep. Guano is a rich fertilizer, and humans have collected it for centuries, sometimes by the shipload. In the late 1800s, many of the Humboldt and African penguins had their nesting sites dug up and removed. Today dried guano is still collected, but in most places enough is left behind for the penguins to dig their burrows.

Penguins that nest in burrows often haul in dried grass, twigs and molted feathers to line the nesting chamber. Cherry Kearton described how African penguins padded their burrows: "I have seen penguins with long, trailing bits of seaweed,

The rocky nest of an Adélie may contain over 1,000 pebbles.

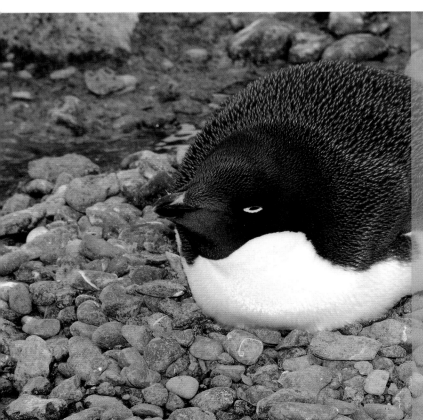

Advantages of Nests

There are definite benefits to building a nest, even when it is only an inch or two high. A nest raises the eggs off the cold, sometimes frozen ground; as a result, the eggs stay warmer. An elevated nest also protects eggs and young chicks from flooding. If the nest is not big enough, however, the meltwater from a late-spring snowstorm can drown chicks and flush eggs right out of the nest.

Penguins use different materials to build their nests: pebbles in gentoos *(top)*, dried grasses in magellanics *(centre)* and clumps of turf in macaronis *(bottom)*.

struggling up the slope from the sea — a matter, as often as not, of half a mile or more — the seaweed becoming entangled in their legs and nearly tripping them up."

Some penguins are not as fussy, and when seaweed and grass are not available, they use whatever trash they can find. In the burrows of magellanic penguins, researchers have uncovered small mammal bones, paper litter, the skulls of songbirds, chips of dried cattle manure, and the dried pelts of dead penguins. Hoping to find something equally interesting, I once crawled down the burrow of a magellanic penguin in the Falkland Islands and found nothing but grass and biting fleas. My interest in penguin burrows ended very quickly.

In the colder climates, most penguins build their nests on top of the ground, because a cool burrow is not necessary to protect young chicks from the heat of the sun. Gentoos in the Falklands gather clumps of earth and construct mounds 6 inches (15 cm) high. On Macquarie Island, one royal penguin made a nest pile entirely of old bleached penguin bones. Adélies and chinstraps are the rock masons of the penguin world, assembling piles of pebbles for their nests.

In the life of a penguin, nest material is valuable, and anything that is valuable is worth stealing. Penguins are incur-

Both southern rockhoppers *(top)* and chinstraps *(bottom)* will steal pebbles from a neighbor's nest any time they can.

able thieves, and a nest owner may be a victim one moment and a robber the next. I have watched penguins steal from each other many times, and it's always entertaining. As soon as a nesting bird nods off for a nap, the neighbors may come calling. A penguin with theft on its mind quietly waddles up to a likely nest. If the nest owner is sleeping or looking in another direction, the pebble pirate slowly leans forward, quickly grabs a stone and then runs off as if its tail is on fire. If the thief gets caught in the act, it may get punished with a hard peck or whacked with a flipper, but that doesn't seem to discourage the culprit. A penguin often tries time and time again until it eventually succeeds. One early penguin researcher painted pebbles bright red and left a pile of them near a colony of Adélies. Within hours the stone stealing started. After three days the red pebbles had been looted from one nest to the next and carried throughout the colony.

In 1995 a trio of Spanish researchers watched stone stealing in a colony of chinstraps and made some interesting discoveries. Although both males and females stole stones from neighboring nests, the males collected larger stones, wandered farther afield to do it and stole more stones than did their female partners. The nests of some pairs tripled in weight during the nesting season, sometimes weighing in at 23 pounds (11 kg) and containing over 600 pebbles. Other nests shrank by as much as 70 percent and contained as few as 36 pebbles. The researchers concluded that experienced, high-ranking males build the largest nests and defended them best. Low-ranking males, on the other hand, can neither defend their nests nor collect enough stones to offset theft by their neighbors.

Two species of penguins, the king and the emperor, never have to worry about having their nests stolen from under them — they simply carry their eggs with them. Both king and emperor females lay a single egg. Within moments, one of the parents rolls the egg onto the top of its feet and covers it with a fold of its feathered belly skin. After that, no matter where the parent moves, the egg is always with it. In king penguins the male and female partners take turns holding and warming the

As in all penguins, mating in gentoos takes just a few seconds, but egg laying may not occur for several weeks afterward.

egg. In emperor penguins the male cradles the egg on his feet for the entire incubation period, which lasts 64 days. The devoted father never lets the egg leave the top of his feet. If ever a penguin deserved the title "Mr. Mom," it's the male emperor.

The Egg Beat

Once two penguins settle down at a nest and steal a few pebbles for each other, they start to get serious, and the mating begins. When you are shaped like a football, that's harder to do than it sounds. While watching several pairs of rockhoppers mate, I recorded these observations in my journal:

> Once the female is sprawled invitingly on her belly, the male hops up onto her back and slowly treads backward — a mounted male reminds me of an excited youngster trying to balance on a skateboard. He nibbles the feathers on his partner's crown and neck, wags his tail from side to side and slaps her flanks with his flippers like a cowboy urging his horse on ... It has been raining for the past couple of days, and all the females have muddy tread marks on their backs.

A penguin pair may start to mate several weeks before the first egg is laid, and as the time of laying draws closer, the birds mount as often as 12 to 14 times a day. Typically, all penguins (except kings and emperors) lay two white eggs, which quickly become stained with mud and guano. Penguin eggs have thicker shells than the eggs of most seabirds; this protects them from the clumsy waddling adults, the beaks of grumpy neighbors and the sharp stones that line many nests.

As mentioned earlier, in all species but emperors, both parents share in incubating the eggs, although the shift schedule differs among the species. With gentoos and the banded penguins, for example, the mates alternate frequently and usually relieve each other every few days. In Adélies, chinstraps and the crested penguins, each sex starts with a long incubation shift lasting between seven and 14 days, after

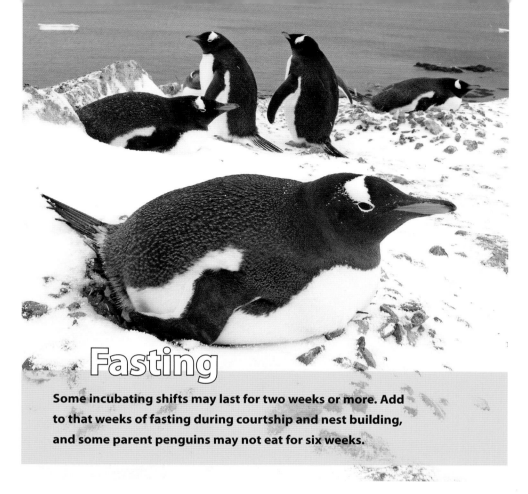

Fasting

Some incubating shifts may last for two weeks or more. Add to that weeks of fasting during courtship and nest building, and some parent penguins may not eat for six weeks.

While incubating, a gentoo in Antarctica burns body fat to keep itself warm.

which the partners change over more frequently as the time of hatching draws closer. In all cases, while one parent incubates, the other heads out to sea to feed and build up its fat reserves again.

One amusing penguin behavior is the "slender walk" of an adult returning to relieve its mate. In large colonies containing several thousand birds, a returning penguin may have to cross the territories of over a hundred bad-tempered neighbors with sharp beaks. All penguin species that nest together in such numbers use this special walk to pass through the crowd with as few pecks and flipper whacks as possible. In Adélies, for example, the bird flattens its feathers to make itself as slim as possible, stretches its flippers behind its back, raises its beak skyward then runs a zigzag course for home. Returning penguins are usually silent, but their body language sends a clear message: just passing through ... sorry to disturb you ... no fights, please.

The urge to incubate must be strong in penguins, because they often nest in very difficult conditions. During a storm in the Falklands, I hiked to a gentoo colony to

Early Days

Newly hatched penguin chicks are covered with fine down ranging from silver gray to dark brown or black, depending on the species. At this age, their eyelids are sealed shut, and like so many young nestlings, they are puny, wobbly-necked bags of fluff that peep constantly to be fed.

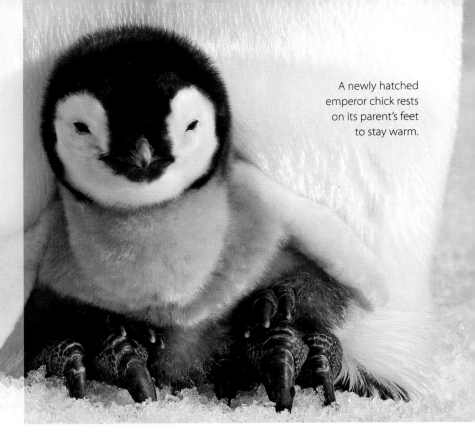

A newly hatched emperor chick rests on its parent's feet to stay warm.

see what the birds have to endure. It was raining hard, and the wind was gusting to 45 miles an hour (70 km/h). The birds sat huddled over their nests, facing into the wind, their eyes closed. What impressed me most was that every bird was completely caked in mud except for its beak.

Snowstorms can be another hardship for penguin parents. On the Antarctic Peninsula, late-spring storms can almost completely bury an incubating bird, leaving only its head visible above the snow. If an Adélie is buried like this for more than three days, the stress is too much for the bird, and it will desert the nest.

The biggest stress for many incubating penguins is the fasting. Remarkably, male emperor penguins may not eat for three months. Incubating birds rely on their fat reserves to provide energy while they are fasting, and they may lose up to half their body weight. These fat reserves can run out, however, and if a mate stays away at sea too long and is late relieving its partner, the incubating bird has no choice but to abandons the eggs and flee to the sea to feed.

Flipper-flapping Fluffies

The eggs of most penguin species hatch after 35 to 40 days. Naturally, it is longer in the two largest species: king penguins incubate for 54 days; emperors, for 64 days. Shortly before an egg begins to crack, the tiny chick can be heard chirping inside the shell. Because the eggshell is so thick, it may take as long as three days for a chick to struggle free. The incubating parents never interfere, although they often look down at the egg and seem very interested in what is happening. Sometimes a parent will even regurgitate gobs of food onto the egg.

During the first weeks of a penguin chick's life, the chick is continuously guarded by one of its parents. Depending on the size of the penguin, the guarding phase lasts anywhere from two to eight weeks. While one parent stands guard, the other hunts for food to feed the cheeping chick. The helpless chick needs to be guarded against three main dangers: the weather, the neighbors and predators.

The temperature on a summer day in Antarctica may be just 40 degrees F (4°C), which is cold enough to kill chicks. The down-feather coat on young chinstraps and Adélies is too thin for them to maintain their own body temperatures. Until they are several weeks old, they huddle under the warmth of a parent's belly fold, stare out and watch the world go by. Penguin chicks grow rapidly, and within a few weeks they have ballooned into potbellied little tubbies that no longer fit under a parent so they simply squat beside the adult bird like miniature Buddhas, waiting to be fed — and fed again.

The weather can still kill young penguins even at this stage in their growth. Cold and blowing snow can freeze the chicks in their tracks. One Christmas in the Falkland Islands, an icy rain battered a southern rockhopper colony for more than 24 hours. Nearly half the chicks in the colony died during the storm. The young penguins, soaked by the rain, were too big for their parents to cover and warm, and when the cold winds drained all their body heat, they froze to death.

Neighbors can sometimes be just as dangerous as the weather. In most colonies there is usually much less squabbling among the adults by the time the chicks begin to hatch. Even so, occasional fights still break out and young nestlings can be injured during the ruckus. A tiny bird can be trampled, punctured with a toenail, kicked and blinded, or knocked from a nest into a neighbor's territory. I watched the fate of one tiny, defenseless southern rockhopper chick that was kicked from its nest while its parent was fighting. I recorded the incident in field notes:

Gentoo penguins *(top)* commonly raise two chicks, whereas southern rockhoppers *(bottom)* rarely raise more than one, even when a second chick hatches.

A crèche of king penguin chicks may contain thousands of youngsters.

"The neighbor adults stretched over and screamed a loud threat at the tiny chick, and then the big-beaked male attacked. He shook the chick vigorously and gave it six or seven hard pecks on the body and head, killing it very quickly. The aggressive male continued to peck at the chick periodically for 10 minutes after it was dead."

Every penguin colony attracts a squad of predators looking for an easy meal. In the Galápagos Islands crimson-shelled Sally Lightfoot crabs will drag off a tiny struggling chick and eat it alive. In Australia there are venomous tiger snakes; in Argentina and Chile, gray foxes and Geoffroy's cats; and in Africa, needle-toothed mongooses. The greatest threat to young penguin chicks, however, is other birds — gulls, skuas and giant petrels — all of which are bold and clever predators. The killing tactics they use will be described in the next chapter.

About a month after hatching, most penguin chicks have grown large enough to be left temporarily on their own. Both parents can now go out to sea and thereby deliver twice as many meals. The behavior of unguarded chicks differs among the various species of penguins. In the burrow- and crevice-nesting banded penguins, the little penguin and white-flippered penguin, the chicks tend to be tiny home-bodies, hanging out by themselves or with their nest mates at the mouth of their burrow. The chicks of most of the other species herd together in sizable groups called "crèches" — gangs of potbellied, flat-footed, flipper-flapping fluffies.

Penguin crèches vary in size. Many of the crested species clump together in groups of 20 to 30 chicks. Downy Adélies can form clusters of 100 or more, and big brown fuzzy king penguin chicks may gather in immense crèches of 1,000 birds. Initially, a crèche may contain just two or three chicks, but it can grow larger very quickly. In one Adélie colony containing several thousand nesting pairs, the first chicks were left unguarded on December 30. Eleven days later, all but 1 percent of the chicks had joined crèches.

When the first chicks in a colony begin to form crèches, there are still many adults guarding smaller chicks. The adults are aggressive around their nests and may peck any careless chick that wanders too near. Because of this, the clusters of chicks usually form on the edge of a colony or, better yet, in an unoccupied area in the center of a colony, where they are surrounded by adult birds that can shield them from predators. Unguarded chicks gather in crèches for two reasons: there is safety in numbers, and a cluster of hot-blooded chicks is a good place to snuggle into when a cold wind blows.

With many species, when a parent returns to the colony to feed its chicks, it may be mobbed by half a dozen hungry beaks. In the past, biologists thought that an adult penguin would feed whichever chick happened to reach it first and beg for food. But now we know that penguins, like just about every other animal on Earth, feed only their own offspring. How does an adult penguin identify its chicks? It listens to the chirps.

Chicks, in turn, memorize the hoarse shrieks of their parents. When a parent penguin returns from the ocean to feed its chicks, it usually goes back to its nest. As it gets close to home, it trumpets and screams that it is coming. As soon a chick hears its parent, it leaves the crèche and hurries back to its old nest to be fed. Curious researchers used tape recordings of adult calls to lure Adélie chicks out of the crèche. In almost every case, the correct Adélie chick — and only that chick — left the security of the crèche and waddled over to the nest.

Chick rearing is the longest part of the nesting cycle and is the time that young penguins as well as their parents are exposed to the greatest danger from predators. In the next chapter you will learn about the enemies of penguins — the ones with feathers; the ones with fur; and the ones with tentacles, flukes and fins.

Of the three brush-tailed penguins, Adélies when nesting crowd the closest to their neighbors.

First Sounds

Penguin chicks begin to chirp even before they are out of the shell — they call all the time. In fact, a parent can quiet a hatched chick only one of two ways: feed it until it bulges, or sit on top of it. At first a chick's voice sounds much like those of the chicks in the surrounding nests. Slowly, however, the chick develops a call different from that of any other chick. For young Adélies this happens by the time the chick is about 3 weeks old. By then the parents have memorized its call, and they remember it for as long as they care for the chick.

55

Penguin Killers

The great white shark is the largest predatory shark in the world.

Gulls are one of the most successful groups of seabirds. There are gulls on every continent and they range from the High Arctic, just 400 miles (645 km) from the North Pole, to the shores of Antarctica. There is usually one species of gull wherever there are penguins. One reason gulls are so successful is that they will eat almost anything, and when they are around penguins, this includes penguin poop, gobs of spilled food, fresh or rotten eggs, dead chicks and defenseless live ones.

The handsome dolphin gull is not big enough to attack a chick, but everything else is fair game. I watched a pair of these gulls work a gentoo colony in the Falkland Islands. Again and again the gulls flew low over the colony, just above the stabbing beaks of the adults, searching for discarded eggs or food that had spilled onto the ground. Another tactic was to walk around the edges of the colony and watch for parents feeding chicks. The crafty gulls sometimes worked together and rushed at the chick just as it was about to receive a gooey gob of food. This frightened the chick, and it often turned away from its parent just as the hot meal was on its way. The bold gulls then grabbed the food right out of the parent's beak or scooped it up as soon as it hit the ground.

The kelp gull is twice as heavy as the dolphin gull and is large enough to attack penguin chicks. A strong flier, the kelp gull can land in the middle of a penguin colony, pick up a small dead chick and fly away before the adults can catch up. The beak and feet of gulls are not designed to kill, so these birds are best at scavenging.

Both the red-billed dolphin gull *(left)* and the larger kelp gull *(right)* have an appetite for penguin eggs and chicks.

The old-time whalers called the giant petrel "stinker," partly because of its taste for rotting carcasses but more because of the seabird's habit of vomiting up foul-smelling stomach oil and spraying it on intruders up to six feet (2 m) away. In the sub-Antarctic islands of New Zealand, I once got too close to a giant petrel chick with my camera, and the chick sprayed my jeans with a jet of oily goo that smelled so bad I had to throw the pants away.

A Stinky Story

The giant petrel is sometimes called the "vulture of the Southern Ocean."

Even so, the adaptable gulls will attack small penguin chicks and any larger chicks that are sick or dying. In South America kelp gulls often patrol colonies of magellanic penguins, looking for unguarded chicks, and in Africa the fearless gulls will even go down into a burrow, drag out a helpless chick and kill it with repeated blows to the head.

Another penguin predator is the giant petrel, a 10-pound (4.5 kg) seabird with a 5-inch (13 cm) butcher beak. This big seabird is large enough to tackle even a full-grown penguin. In Argentina a researcher watched the struggle between a giant petrel and an adult magellanic penguin. The battle lasted for nearly 15 minutes, until finally, the exhausted petrel drowned the penguin. A magellanic penguin weighs as much as a petrel and is armed with an equally dangerous beak. As a result, such daring attacks on healthy adult penguins are probably quite rare.

It is a different story if the penguin is sick or injured. Many times I have seen one or more giant petrels lying quietly on the beach near a bloodied penguin, waiting for the penguin to weaken enough for an attack. Such was the case in South Georgia when I spent an hour watching as five giant petrels surrounded an injured macaroni penguin. The penguin was soaked in blood from a severe laceration on its neck and did not look as if it would survive. Even though the penguin was very weak, the petrels did not attack it. When some tourists landed and accidentally frightened the injured macaroni into the water, the stinkers swarmed over the dying bird and tore it apart. Minutes later, nothing was left but the penguin's feathered skin and a pair of pink feet floating on the swell.

Skuas: Seabirds of Prey

Skuas look like gulls and are closely related to them, but they behave more like birds of prey. Their beaks are sharp edged and hooked; they have curved claws on their webbed feet; and their legs are covered with tough, protective scales. Seabird expert Robert Cushman Murphy admired the skuas he saw on South Georgia, writing that "the skuas look and act like miniature eagles. They fear nothing, [and] never seek to avoid being conspicuous, and by every token of their behavior, they are Lords of the Far South."

Skuas pester penguins more than any other birds do, stealing their eggs and preying on their chicks. For five years researcher Dr. Euan Young studied the hunting tactics of a group of skuas in a colony of nesting Adélie penguins. The stealthy skuas used three main methods to outwit the penguins. In a "jump attack," the skua, with wings raised, rushes and leaps at a standing penguin, striking it high on the body with its outstretched feet and knocking the bird off balance. In the excitement an egg or small chick may be uncovered, and the fast-acting skua nabs it before the penguin can react.

A bolder maneuver is the "crash flight." Here, a skua glides into a penguin. The force of the collision may knock the startled penguin into its irritable neighbors, adding to the commotion. Although both the jump attack and the crash flight are successful roughly one-third of the

Top: A brown skua scavenges a dead king penguin.

Bottom: A gentoo chases away a scavenging skua before feeding its chick.

time, they expose the skua to the high risk of injury, so neither method is used very often. If a couple of penguins manage to grab a skua, they can do some serious damage. The penguin's stiff flippers are strong enough to break bones, and its beak is a dangerous weapon. I once watched an unfortunate skua drop into the middle of a southern rockhopper colony and try to snatch a small chick. It caught the chick, but then the penguins caught the skua. Half a dozen rockhoppers attacked, viciously beating it with their bony flippers and tearing at its head and body with their powerful beaks. The skua dropped the penguin chick almost immediately but was unable to get away because there were too many penguins pulling at its body for it to get airborne. The bird's only choice was to struggle on foot to the edge of the colony, fighting off new attackers every few feet. When the battered skua finally escaped, its left wing was drooping and it had blood on the feathers of its face. The final score for the day: penguins 1, skua 0.

The more common, and safer, skua hunting tactic is to tug on a nesting penguin's tail feathers. When the bird swivels to respond, its chicks or eggs are exposed to attack. This method works even better when two skuas team up. While one bird pesters the penguin, the other grabs lunch. If a skua catches a penguin snoozing, it can sometimes jerk its tail feathers so strongly that the sleeping bird is pulled off the nest. Before the surprised penguin can react, the skua leaps over and grabs an egg or a chick.

Fin-footed Hunters

Seals, sea lions and fur seals — the fin-footed mammals — inhabit every ocean on Earth. All are carnivores and hunt for a living, and for some of them, penguins are on the menu. No sea lion or fur seal is a full-time penguin killer, but in many areas they may hunt penguins when an opportunity arises.

All the fin-footed mammals, such as the South America sea lion *(bottom)*, leopard seal *(top)* and Antarctic fur seal *(middle)*, evolved from a weasel-like ancestor.

How Predators Hunt

During the nesting season, adult penguins move back and forth from their colonies to the ocean every few days, if not more often. After they return from long feeding trips, the birds are tired, weighted down with food and easier to catch. Sea lions and fur seals, especially juvenile males, often station themselves offshore from large penguin colonies and hunt the birds, not only for food but sometimes also for sport.

Adélie penguins behave nervously before entering the water.

I watched a young male South American sea lion catch and kill two king penguins on a beach in the Falkland Islands. Although the sea lion ate part of the first penguin, it ate none of the second. The animal played in the surf with the second king for several minutes, even tossing the flapping bird into the air. Once the penguin was dead, the sea lion submerged with the bird's body in its mouth a couple of times and then abandoned the carcass. A dozen giant petrels, attracted by the commotion in the water, made certain that no scrap was wasted.

The fin-footed penguin killer that ranks above all others is the 900-pound (400 kg) leopard seal of the Antarctic. In one year a dozen leopard seals hunting at the large Adélie colony at Cape Crozier killed 4,800 adults and 1,200 chicks. Young penguins moving into the water on their first trip to sea are easy prey; they are literally sitting penguins. The inexperienced Adélies are completely unaware of the danger from a leopard seal. A curious youngster may even swim over to a seal that is floating quietly on the surface. *Snap.* Another lesson learned.

Adult Adélies are much warier and harder to catch. Even so, leopard seals in

An Adélie penguin never wants to be left behind when a group leaves.

some areas manage to kill 5 percent of the adult penguins in a colony. That doesn't sound like very many penguins, until you remember that some colonies have 200,000 breeding birds. The leopard seal toll at one of those colonies would be 10,000 penguins.

Leopard seals use a number of strategies to hunt penguins. One is to stalk the birds from under thin ice. With this method an underwater seal follows a penguin walking across newly formed ice, breaks through the ice (which can be up to 3 inches/7.5 cm thick) and grabs the unsuspecting bird. If a penguin spots a seal before it attacks, the bird may freeze with fear then remain motionless for over an hour until it feels safe to continue.

Leopard seals also leap onto ice floes and try to snatch any careless penguin that is standing near the edge. If no penguin is close enough to catch, the seal may attempt to drive the birds off the safety of the ice and then pursue them in an underwater chase.

One popular hunting method is for a seal to lie quietly facing out to sea in the water near shore where it is hidden between pieces of floating ice. Returning penguins literally swim into the seal's jaws. The most common technique is for a leopard seal to patrol an ice edge where the penguins must leap up out of the water and onto the ice in order to reach shore. When the tide is out, the ice edge may be 5 feet (1.5 m) high, and the birds may have to make many leaps before they succeed. The tired penguins are easy targets.

Penguins are not defenseless. To begin with, they are sharp-sighted, accomplished divers that are more at home underwater than any other seabird. This alone gives them a great advantage. Furthermore, they have a few tricks to stack the odds in their favor. Whenever penguins leave or return to a colony, they travel in groups — the bigger, the better. A group of penguins is more likely to spot an approaching seal, so there is less chance of a surprise attack. As well, an individual bird fleeing in a group is less likely to be singled out by a predator. Another way penguins outwit their enemies is by porpoising. As we saw earlier, a porpoising penguin is more difficult for an underwater seal to track and follow. Many penguins swim this way whenever they are close to shore and predators are lurking. Finally, penguins swimming near their colonies stay as quiet as possible and save the noisy squawks and screams until they are back at their nests.

A curious king penguin may sometimes nibble playfully on a fur seal pup.

A great white shark has roughly 300 teeth, arranged in many rows.

Sharks!

In warmer waters barracuda and sharks also prey on penguins. In one colony of African penguins, for example, nearly half the birds had lacerations on their feet and flippers. Eight species of sharks inhabit the offshore waters, but researchers believe the toothy culprit is likely the great white shark, the same predator known to attack human surfers off the beaches of California and Australia.

More Hungry Mouths

On a warm, sunny afternoon one December, I watched the shoreline where the members of a mixed colony of gentoos and magellanic penguins were landing. I wrote this in my journal:

> I never saw the killer whales until they were very close to shore. There were four, maybe five animals in the pod, including a large adult male with a 6-foot-high (2 m) dorsal fin. The orcas were swimming slowly through a thick forest of giant kelp just offshore. Suddenly, one of the whales rushed forward, and ahead of it, half a dozen gentoo penguins porpoised to the surface as if they had been shot from a cannon. One of the whales spouted in a swirl of white water then dove. When the penguins appeared next, they were spread out and porpoising rapidly toward the shore. Moments later, individual birds began to pop safely out of the waves hitting the beach. The drama ended as fast as it began, and the whales disappeared around the point.

Killer whales probably hunt the larger species of penguins — the kings and emperors — more often than they do the smaller ones. The Crozet Islands, south of the Indian Ocean, are home to over 735,000 pairs of breeding king penguins, nearly half the world's population. French researchers have for many years been studying the pods of orcas that live around these islands, and they have frequently watched the black-and-white killers hunt and catch the kings. They have even seen a whale play with a live king as if it were a toy, tossing the bird into the air with its mouth and then leaping clear of the water and batting the penguin with a blow from its tail.

Young African penguins must sometimes deal with the most unexpected predator of all. In 1930 Cherry Kearton wrote this dramatic and colorful description:

> The young penguin [African] meets his next enemies as soon as he goes to sea ... The penguin, floating probably and as yet barely able to swim, strays from the maternal care, out to the deeper water and close to rocks that overhang the most inviting pools. The octopus ... with tentacles outstretched [waits] for whatever may come within its reach. And then — a vice-like grip on dangling legs — a sudden pull, against which it is impossible to struggle — and one more penguin has disappeared.

The light patches on Antarctic killer whales are yellow tinged rather than the usual white.

Parting
Penguins

Hungry chinstrap chicks will beg for food from any adult that wanders near them.

For most penguin chicks, family life reaches an end in January and February, the middle weeks of the southern summer. Typically, the family breaks up fairly quickly. Over a week or two, first one parent stops its feeding visits then the other. At this stage the chicks are 2 to 4 months old, and many are nearly as big as their parents.

The young penguins no longer huddle in crèches; they either cluster in small groups at the edge of the colonies or hang out near the shoreline, watching the waves of adults come and go. Many of them are molting the last of the fluffy down they had as chicks, and they look quite comical. Tufts of down sprout from the tops of their heads like punk hairdos, and wispy strands still cling to their necks like the fur collar on a winter coat. A chick's down feathers don't shed water the way the feathers of an adult do, and if a youngster wanders too close to the ocean and gets wet, the down hangs on its body in great soggy clumps, making it look even more comical.

It is at this age that curious young penguins begin to explore their world. Southern elephant seals share many beaches with penguins, and the seals haul out to molt at just about the time that penguin chicks are leaving home. A 14-foot (4 m), 9,000-pound (4 100 kg) bull elephant seal sprawled on the beach must be an irresistible temptation for a chick to investigate. On Macquarie Island, I watched

A squid-eating southern elephant seal poses no danger to king penguins.

A molting gentoo chick waits near the shore for a parent to return.

a young king penguin nibble at the hind flipper of an elephant seal then squawk in fright and flee as soon as the sluggish seal lifted its head and belched. One adventurous chick even climbed on top of one of these monster beach slugs and, for a brief moment, was lord of its universe. The seal arched up in annoyance, however, and the startled penguin tumbled off and hit the beach with its flippers and feet spinning in high gear.

Some of my best penguin experiences have been with young birds of this age. Often, I have sat quietly and let the youngsters waddle over and check me out. An experience I recorded in my field notes about a gang of young gentoos was fairly typical:

Within a few minutes, six or seven nearly full-grown chicks rocked their way over to investigate. As they approached, they craned their necks in every conceivable direction, seemingly trying to figure out what kind of creature I was. After each bout of neck stretching, they shuffled ahead a few steps and repeated the inspection. If I moved suddenly, the penguins squawked in alarm, ran back a few steps, stopped and looked at me over their shoulders. In a few moments their courage returned, and they eased toward me once more. Eventually, one bold chick, the largest in the group, tugged at the sleeve of my jacket. Satisfied that I was neither tasty nor dangerous, the daring chick turned away and waddled off with its companions. Clearly, there were more interesting discoveries to be made in life.

Chick Checkout

Some early penguin researchers believed that chicks stayed ashore until starvation finally forced them into the ocean. Others thought that the parents lured their young into the water and taught them to swim before the family broke up. Neither of these beliefs has proved correct. In fact there are no last-minute swimming lessons with a parent and no adult bird feeds its chicks at sea. The young birds leave without their parents, although they may follow a group of adults. Many still have food in their stomachs, so it is unlikely that they have gone without eating for very long before they leave. In crowded beach areas, some chicks are simply shoved into

Chicks are clumsy swimmers and unaware of the danger from killer whales, sea lions and leopard seals. As we have seen, when so many young penguins leave at the same time, the local predators are flooded with more easy prey than they can hunt. As a result, even though the predators capture many chicks, many more chicks escape and make it to the open sea.

Survivors by the Numbers

Young magellanic penguins lack the distinctive chest band present in adults.

the water accidentally when a group of adults leaves for the sea, or they are washed off the rocks by an unexpected wave.

No matter how or why a young penguin finally takes the plunge, once the chicks in a colony begin to leave they all leave in a very short time. Researchers counted the chicks in an Adélie colony in the Ross Sea of Antarctica. On January 27 all the chicks in the colony were still ashore, loafing along the shoreline. Within three days the first chicks began to leave, and after a week half of them were gone. Within two weeks every chick had left. At some large colonies 50,000 chicks may leave within a one-week period.

Once the young penguins reach the sea, there are no more free lunches. They must feed themselves for the first time. And if they thought their parents made them run for lunch in the colony, wait until they see how fast krill, fish and squid can move. Two events make a chick's first trip to sea a little easier to manage. First, the timing of chick departure often coincides with the peak of food production in the oceans where penguins live. The days are the longest of the year, plankton

Young gentoo chicks will huddle for safety.

growth is at its maximum and food is abundant, so even inexperienced penguin chicks can usually catch enough to eat. The timing also coincides with the annual molting period, when most of the adult birds in the colony are forced to stay ashore for up to a month or more. So for at least a few weeks the chicks do not have to compete with experienced adults for food. By the time the adults return to the sea, the chicks are better at finding and catching their meals and better able to compete.

Fat for Feathers

Every activity in a penguin's life takes energy, especially these three: reproduction, migration and molting. For penguins, molting takes by far the most. At the end of the breeding season, the adults go out to sea to feast and fatten. Sometimes they may need only three weeks to plumpen up, sometimes three months. When they finally return to shore, they are the fattest they will be at any time of the year. Some may be so padded that they can barely climb up the beach to reach a resting spot. The majority of penguins return to their breeding colonies to molt. The two most polar species, Adélies and emperors, usually stay on the sea ice, or hop aboard an iceberg and float while they molt.

Most penguin species spend two to four weeks replacing their feathers, but the large kings and emperors may require four to six weeks. A penguin fasts for the entire molting period and it may lose half its body weight. Other aquatic birds, such as ducks and geese, may become flightless when they molt, but none lose all their feathers at once, and none are forced to stay out of water, as are penguins. There are a couple of good reasons that the molting pattern in penguins is so different from that of other birds. To begin with, if a penguin goes into the water while it is molting, it can lose excessive amounts of body heat and its temperature may drop. When researchers immersed a molting Galápagos penguin in water at 70 degrees F (21°C), the bird's body temperature dropped 10 Fahrenheit degrees (5.5C°) in just 30 seconds.

Another reason for a molting penguin to stay ashore is that its frayed plumage destroys its streamlined profile, slowing the bird down and making it more vulnerable to predators. As well, a slower penguin might burn up more energy hunting than it gains by eating what it catches.

The molting period for most penguin species is the final event in the breeding season. After this more than half the species migrate to sea and disappear for six months or more, until they return once again the following spring to their crowded colonies — the "ancient graveyards" of their ancestors.

It takes several weeks for a king penguin chick *(top)* or an Adélie chick *(bottom)* to molt and lose their baby feathers.

Problems in Penguinland

Every year, magellanic penguins in South America die when oil spills soil their feathers.

I

n the 1980s, conservationists were worried about the survival of only three species of penguin: African, Humboldt and Galápagos. In the 1990s, their concerns grew when five species were in trouble. In 2013, an international meeting of penguin experts agreed that 12 species were either threatened, vulnerable or endangered. Clearly, penguins are in peril. The five biggest threats they face are oil pollution, habitat destruction, introduced predators, overfishing and — the most dangerous threat of all — global warming and climate change.

The oil pollution impacting penguins can come from several sources. For example, when an oil tanker, some of them three times longer than a football field, runs aground and leaks gallons of oil into the ocean, many penguins can be affected. This happened in 2011 on Tristan da Cunha Island, in the southern Atlantic Ocean, when thousands of endangered northern rockhopper penguins were coated with oil and died. Oil can also come from a ship's holding tanks when a captain illegally rinses them with seawater and then empties the oily water into the ocean.

Oil causes a penguin's feathers to clump, which lessens their insulating ability, and a penguin soon dies if it loses too much body heat. A penguin may also swallow oil accidentally when it preens soiled feathers, and oil is poisonous.

Habitat destruction is another threat facing penguins. Humans can carelessly destroy coastal areas important for nesting penguins and the birds often have no place

African penguins are endangered and declining.

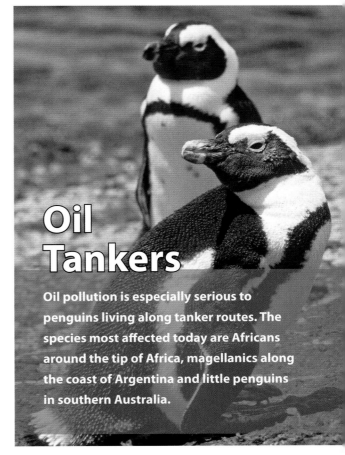

Oil Tankers

Oil pollution is especially serious to penguins living along tanker routes. The species most affected today are Africans around the tip of Africa, magellanics along the coast of Argentina and little penguins in southern Australia.

The yellow-eyed penguin is critically endangered; fewer than 2,000 pairs remain.

else to go. This occurs mainly in penguins living close to areas with large human populations. The yellow-eyed penguins of New Zealand are a good example where this has happened.

Humans can not only destroy important penguin habitat but also accidentally introduce unwanted predators, such as rats and domestic cats. Penguins, like many seabirds, use nesting islands where normally there are no such predators. Unfortunately, hungry cats and rats are dangerous mammals. Cats will kill adult penguins, as well as their chicks, and rats have a great taste for penguin eggs and unguarded nestlings. The impact from the teeth and claws of such animals is an important cause of declines among yellow-eyed and fiordland penguins in New Zealand and little penguins in Australia.

As the human population has slowly increased (currently over seven billion), so has the drive to catch more and more fish. Today fishing boats scour every corner of every ocean. Many target the same schooling fish (anchovies and sardines) that are the principal food of countless penguins. Invariably, when wildlife and humans compete, humans win and wildlife suffers. Overfishing by humans along the west coasts of South America and Africa have caused declines in both Humboldt and African penguins respectively. For the same reason, southern rockhopper numbers have decreased greatly in the Falkland Islands. As well as declines from overfishing, great numbers of penguins also die from drowning when they accidentally become tangled in fishing nets.

The World Is Warming Up

Since I was born, more than 60 years ago, our planet has warmed by 1.5 Fahrenheit degrees (0.8°C). That doesn't sound like very much, but the consequences have been serious. To begin with, the warming has not been even throughout the world. Whereas tropical areas have warmed very little, the ice- and snow-covered polar regions, namely the Arctic and the Antarctic, have warmed up a lot. The Antarctic Peninsula, home to millions of penguins, has warmed the most. On the peninsula, the average temperature has increased by 6 Fahrenheit degrees (3.5°C) and the midwinter temperatures have warmed by a remarkable 11 Fahrenheit degrees (6°C). Such added warmth has had a dramatic impact on the penguins that live there.

Warmer winter temperatures in the Antarctic mean less sea ice — in fact, as much as 40 percent less. Sea ice is an important nursery area for krill and Antarctic silverfish. Both are important foods for nesting chinstrap and Adélie penguins. As krill and silverfish populations have declined, so have the numbers of these penguins. In some areas of the peninsula, Adélie colonies have shrunk by 80 to 90 percent.

Less Antarctic sea ice also means there is more open water to create clouds. More clouds result in greater spring snowfall and more blizzards. Such spring storms can blanket Adélie and chinstrap colonies in deep snow just when the penguins are laying eggs and feeding chicks. If the snow is too deep, the birds abandon their nests. Even if the snow melts quickly, the resulting flood can flush eggs away and drown tiny chicks.

Warmer temperatures in the Antarctic are a threat to emperors, as well, the only penguin species that nests directly on the sea ice. When the ice disappears too soon in early summer, the penguins don't have enough time to finish their breeding cycle. An entire season of down-covered chicks can die when they get dumped into icy water before they have an insulating coat of feathers.

Beyond the Antarctic, warmer temperatures also affect global climate patterns. One of these patterns is El Niño. Every three to seven years, warm water in the western Pacific floods eastward toward South America, displacing the cold coastal currents that normally support many seabirds, including Humboldt and Galápagos penguins. During an El Niño year the penguins stop breeding because fish are scarce in the warm water. In a really bad year even adults may starve to death. During the severe El Niño of 1982–83, for example, nearly 80 percent of Galápagos penguins died.

Penguins are a remarkable family of birds that have been on Earth since the Age of Dinosaurs. My only hope for their future is perhaps expressed best by the words of veteran penguin researcher Dr. Bernard Stonehouse, who wrote, "I have had the impression that to penguins, man is just another penguin — different, less predictable, occasionally violent, but tolerable company when he sits still and minds his own business."

This Adélie penguin eventually abandoned its nest because of the deep snow.

75

Penguins of the World

1

Northern Rockhopper
(Eudyptes moseleyi)

2

Southern Rockhopper
(Eudyptes chrysocome)

3

Eastern Rockhopper
(Eudyptes filholi)

4

Fiordland
(Eudyptes pachyrhynchus)

5

Snares
(Eudyptes robustus)

6

Erect-crested
(Eudyptes sclateri)

7

Macaroni
(Eudyptes chrysolophus)

8

Royal
(Eudyptes schlegeli)

9

Magellanic
(Spheniscus magellanicus)

10

Humboldt
(Spheniscus humboldti)

11

Galápagos
(Spheniscus mendiculus)

12

African
(Spheniscus demersus)

13

Adélie
(Pygoscelis adeliae)

14

Chinstrap
(Pygoscelis antarctica)

15

Gentoo
(Pygoscelis papua)

16

Emperor
(Aptenodytes forsteri)

17

King
(Aptenodytes patagonicus)

18

Yellow-eyed
(Megadyptes antipodes)

19

Little
(Eudyptula minor)

20

White-flippered
(Eudyptula albosignata)

Note: page numbers in **bold** refer to pictures.

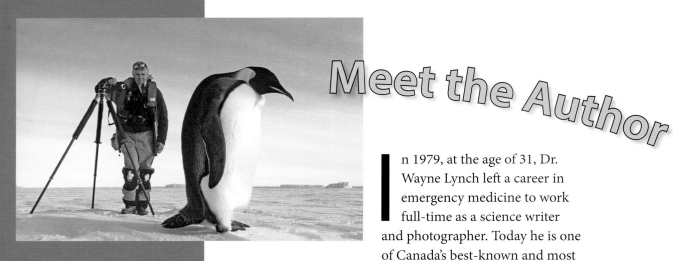

I n 1979, at the age of 31, Dr. Wayne Lynch left a career in emergency medicine to work full-time as a science writer and photographer. Today he is one of Canada's best-known and most widely published professional wildlife photographers. His photo credits include hundreds of magazine covers, thousands of calendar shots and tens of thousands of images published in over 70 countries. He is also the author and photographer of over a dozen highly acclaimed natural history books for adults, including *Penguins of the World*; *Bears: Monarchs of the Northern Wilderness*; *A is for Arctic: Natural Wonders of a Polar World*; *Married to the Wind: A Study of the Prairie Grasslands*; *Planet Arctic: Life at the Top of the World*; *The Great Northern Kingdom: Life in the Boreal Forest*; and *Owls of the United States and Canada: A Complete Guide to Their Biology and Behavior*. His books have been described as "a magical combination of words and images."

Dr. Lynch has observed and photographed wildlife in over 60 countries and is a Fellow of the internationally recognized Explorers Club, headquartered in New York City. A Fellow is someone who has actively participated in exploration or has substantially enlarged the scope of human knowledge through scientific achievements and published reports, books and articles. In 1997 Dr. Lynch was elected as a Fellow to the Arctic Institute of North America, in recognition of his contributions to the knowledge of polar and subpolar regions.

Further Reading

Borboroglu, P. G., and P. D. Boersma, eds. *Penguins: Natural History and Conservation*. Seattle: University of Washington Press, 2013.

Gaston, A. J. *Seabirds: A Natural History*. New Haven: Yale University Press, 2004.

Hooper, M. *The Ferocious Summer: Adélie Penguins and the Warming of Antarctica*. Vancouver: Greystone Books, 2008.

Kooyman G. L., and W. Lynch. *Penguins: The Animal Answer Guide*. Baltimore: Johns Hopkins University Press, 2013.

Lynch, W. *Penguins of the World*. Richmond Hill: Firefly Books, 2007.

Montaigne, F. *Fraser's Penguins: Warning Signs from Antarctica*. New York: St. Martin's Griffin, 2010.